MW00448396

The
Gratitude
Effect
Positivity
Journal

The Gratitude Effect

Positivity Journal

90 Days to Rewire Your Brain

Randy E. Kamen, EdD

ZEITGEIST · NEW YORK

90-Day Gratitude Tracker

Consistency is key when nurturing positivity. Mark off each day to track your progress.

I commit to

I want to do this because

1	2	3	4	5	6	7	8	9	10
11	12	13	14	15	16	17	18	19	20
21	22	23	24	25	26	27	28	29	30
31	32	33	34	35	36	37	38	39	40
41	42	43	44	45	46	47	48	49	50
51	52	53	54	55	56	57	58	59	60
61	62	63	64	65	66	67	68	69	70
71	72	73	74	75	76	77	78	79	80
81	82	83	84	85	86	87	88	89	90

This publication contains the opinions and ideas of its author. It is intended to provide helpful and informative material on the subject matter covered. It is sold with the understanding that the author and publisher are not engaged in rendering professional services in the book. If the reader requires personal assistance or advice, a competent professional should be consulted. The author and publisher specifically disclaim any responsibility for any liability, loss, or risk, personal or otherwise, which is incurred as a consequence, directly or indirectly, of the use and application of any of the contents of this book.

Copyright © 2023 by Penguin Random House LLC

All rights reserved.

Published in the United States by Zeitgeist, an imprint of Zeitgeist™, a division of Penguin Random House LLC, New York.

zeitgeistpublishing.com

Zeitgeist™ is a trademark of Penguin Random House LLC

ISBN: 9780593690062

Illustration © by Ron Dale/Shutterstock.com
Book design by Aimee Fleck
Author photograph © by Nikki Incandela
Edited by Clara Song Lee

Printed in the United States of America
1st Printing

To my children, Amy and Max,
for whom I have infinite gratitude

Contents

How to Use This Journal

Research shows that regularly practicing gratitude creates lasting changes in the brain that promote positive thinking and improved health and well-being in myriad ways—what I call "the gratitude effect." We can train our brain to feel more positive emotions like joy, optimism, and pleasure while simultaneously reducing stress and anxiety, building resilience to adversity, and strengthening our immune system, cardiac health, sleep hygiene, and more.

Even a daily five-minute gratitude practice can strengthen your capacity for positive thinking, and because the effects of gratitude are cumulative, the more you practice, the greater its impact over time.

Cultivating a Gratitude Habit

The first part of this journal explains the science behind gratitude and positive thinking and the remarkable ways they improve our health and well-being. It also includes practical tips and strategies to support a gratitude habit that extends beyond the pages of this journal, including:

- Strategies to overcome negativity bias (page 18)

- Tips to overcome pessimism (page 23)

- Instructions for reframing negative thoughts (page 24)

- Powerful advice and examples for setting intentions (page 28)

- Gratitude practices that supplement daily journaling (page 32)
- A guided gratitude meditation (page 33)
- A Hawaiian prayer that supports healing (page 34)
- Journaling prompts to get gratitude flowing (page 35)

While these tips and strategies are incredibly helpful for cultivating gratitude, they are not required reading. Feel free to skip to the next part if you want to dive right in to the heart of your work—the journaling practice.

Keeping a Gratitude Journal

Commit to writing in your gratitude journal regularly, even if it's only for a few minutes a day. You can use the gratitude tracker on page 5 to keep yourself accountable and motivated. Here are some additional tips to make the most of your journaling practice:

Minimize obstacles. Set yourself up for success by scheduling time to write in your journal, ideally at the same time and place each day, and make sure everything you need is ready to go when you sit down to write.

Prioritize consistency. Pick a time when you're most likely to stay committed, and start small. Short but consistent journal entries are better than lengthy ones. If you miss a day, no worries. Be kind to yourself and resume the next day.

Relax before journaling. Sit comfortably with your body in good alignment and take three to four deep breaths, exhaling fully each time. This will allow your thoughts and feelings to flow more readily.

Be as specific as possible. When describing your experiences, allow yourself to dive deeper and explore the nuances of these moments and events. Research shows that including details strengthens the effects of gratitude journaling.

Don't censor yourself. Listen to your heart and share whatever feels moving or positive in some way. Your journal is for you alone, and it can be as personal, intimate, or messy as you need or want it to be.

Allow creativity to flow. Some people find that expressing gratitude through images, doodles, or sketching enhances their journaling. Write or draw whatever feels right.

If you ever feel stumped, check out the gratitude prompts on page 35 to elicit positive memories, associations, and experiences. You can also use the reframing skill on page 24 to access new perspectives about negative thoughts you may have.

The Power of Positive Thinking

> **66** In reality, the simplest and most practical way to rewire your brain for positive thinking is to take time to reflect, be grateful, and be aware of the positive things in your life."
>
> —**Mark Hoelterhoff, PhD,** *positive psychology expert at the University of Edinburgh*

As a psychologist who has spent decades working in the field of mind-body medicine and positive psychology, I've known for years how beneficial gratitude can be for cultivating resilience in the face of adversity. I've studied the research on how gratitude helps improve mental, emotional, and physical health. But it wasn't until 2022, when I was involved in a serious bicycle accident and hospitalized for a spinal cord and traumatic brain injury, that my beliefs were put to the test.

A year later, I'm incredibly grateful to report that my back and brain's recovery has surpassed all medical expectations. The healing process has been slow, challenging, and often painful, but I credit my gratitude practices and positive thinking for supporting powerful, beneficial changes in my mind and body.

Since being blessed with this new lease on life, I feel renewed passion for teaching others about gratitude. I hope this journal helps you improve your life in profound and meaningful ways.

The Gratitude Effect

Gratitude is a powerful emotion that conveys appreciation for a moment or experience that has touched us in some way and for which we feel moved to express thankfulness. When we experience and express gratitude, the brain releases neurotransmitters such as dopamine and serotonin, resulting in a host of tangible benefits associated with positive thinking and emotions. We feel more joyful, optimistic, energized, and connected to others. We experience diminished stress, anxiety, depression, and pain. We also build a stronger immune system, have better cardiac health, sleep better, and are more likely to exercise. *This* is the gratitude effect at work.

Moreover, when we communicate gratitude to one another, we are essentially saying, "I see you and I appreciate you." Remarkably, both the person giving thanks and the person receiving thanks experience benefits from this seemingly little exchange.

Unfortunately, most of us are lacking in the appreciation department and continue to focus on all that has gone wrong and what we fear might go wrong. Even when we want to flip the switch and start adopting a more positive and grateful attitude, it can be extremely difficult to do so, especially if we don't know how to make this happen. This is where learning about the brain's ability to change and adapt can help.

Change Your Focus to Change Your Brain

We have all witnessed the rapid brain growth that happens during the first few years of a child's life. Research shows that although this process slows down in adulthood, it continues to occur throughout life. As we learn and gain new experiences, some neural connections are strengthened while others are minimized or eliminated, a process called synaptic pruning. This ability to create new neural pathways and alter or reinforce existing ones is known as neuroplasticity, or brain plasticity; it refers to the brain's ability to change and adapt as a result of our experiences—both positive and negative.

In 1949, Donald Hebb, often referred to as the father of neuropsychology, famously said, "Neurons that fire together, wire together." In other words, the brain reinforces what we repeatedly focus on. With that in mind, it behooves us to deliberately adjust our thoughts, feelings, and behaviors to hardwire positive memories and experiences into the brain.

By practicing gratitude regularly, we proactively train our brains to notice the good in life. In doing so, we build a foundation of positive memories and experiences. We can then draw upon this wealth of positivity to boost and support us when difficulties arise. Over time, we learn to become better observers of the good in our lives and simultaneously become more appreciative—and when the inevitable losses and challenges come along, we have internalized resources to draw upon.

Because of the brain's extraordinary capacity to continue to grow and strengthen new neural networks, it is possible to change our mindset, even despite genetics, past trauma, or life circumstances. But to do so, we must first learn how to overcome certain propensities we have inherited from our ancestors.

The Negativity Bias

In prehistoric times, people lived in a perpetual state of high alert. Threats arose from competing and warring neighbors, environmental circumstances, food scarcity, and more. To avoid danger, one needed to be ever vigilant to survive and protect one's family. While there are reasons to be mindful of our surroundings today, most of us do not live with perpetual threats looming in our immediate environment. Yet, through evolution, we remain hardwired to focus on our worst fears or upsetting scenarios. This is known as the negativity bias.

However, we now know that when we collect a "library" of positive mental images, memories, and emotions, we can offset the heaviness of the negativity bias. This is because our feeling states are partly governed by the amygdala, a tiny structure deep inside the brain responsible for processing positive and negative emotions. A recent study from MIT found that our emotions are controlled by two sets of neurons that genetically encode memories of either pleasurable or fearful situations. These two sets of neurons inhibit each other, suggesting that an imbalance between them in favor of the fearful set may be responsible for disorders such as depression, anxiety, and post-traumatic stress disorder.

Fortunately, building up our stores of positive memories, images, and feelings supports us in addressing the imbalance that the negativity bias predisposes us to. What's more, these don't have to be monumental occurrences. For example, it helps to notice tiny positive moments that bring small spikes of joy—what licensed social worker Deb Dana calls "glimmers" in *The Polyvagal Theory in Therapy*. Glimmers are small, easy-to-miss moments that spark peace or joy, such as your first sip of coffee in the morning or the sound of a cat purring on your lap. The next time you notice a glimmer, allow yourself to savor the sweetness.

Here are some other strategies for overcoming negativity bias. Choose one or two to focus on at a time:

- Set aside some protected time each day for self-care by doing something good for your body.

- Commit to a morning ritual that supports a good beginning to your day. Even a few deep breaths and setting an intention will cast a positive tone (see page 21). Morning rituals get easier to practice over time.

- Practice reframing (see page 24). Recognize and identify negative thoughts and negative self-talk. Ask yourself if these are true or helpful. If not, replace them with words and phrases that are more advantageous and supportive. Research shows that reframing helps support a positive mindset, which can increase productivity and satisfaction and reduce mistakes.

- Keep an active gratitude journal. Being aware of gifts, support, kindnesses, blessings, and other people's generosity strengthens your ability to reframe negative thoughts into positive ones.

- Scan the horizon for all that *is* working and going well in your life and the world, rather than scanning for what *isn't* working, which we do unconsciously.

- Connect daily with someone you are grateful to have in your life.

- Eliminate negative influences wherever possible. This includes avoiding the morning news. Research shows that three minutes of negative news in the morning significantly increases your chances of having negative experiences during the day.

- Instead of engaging in gossip, share positive stories with friends, colleagues, or family members about what's going well and what you are grateful for.

Dr. Kamen's Simple Success Strategy

I encourage everyone I teach to set aside a few minutes several times a day to retrain the brain so that it becomes their best advocate. If possible, attach these actions to existing behaviors so the new habits stick more easily. For example, do your morning ritual after you brush your teeth, or scan the horizon for something good right after you finish your lunch. The following routine has served me incredibly well. Feel free to adopt it as your own!

- Start with a morning ritual. Take four deep breaths, making sure to exhale completely each time, and then set your intention for the day (3 to 5 minutes).
- Later that day, scan the horizon for something good, no matter how brief or insignificant. Savor that positive moment or experience to internalize it (1 to 3 minutes).
- End the day with gratitude journaling. Jot down notes or free write about moments for which you're grateful, then embellish upon one of those experiences. At the bare minimum, don't go to bed without saying aloud what you're grateful for (3 to 5 minutes).

Mindset is a choice but not always an easy one. You have ultimate control over the way you show up to work, in your relationships, and most importantly for yourself. Remember that we can't stop all negative thoughts from arising, and they can serve a purpose when true threats arise. However, most of us stand to benefit immensely by building a greater repertoire of positive thoughts and experiences.

Please note: Everything in this journal is about training your brain to be your own best advocate so you can move through life's ups and downs more skillfully; it is not about engaging in "toxic positivity," which is the pressure to feel or display positive emotions while in the throes of a difficult or painful situation. Toxic positivity is destructive and can lead to more suffering, isolation, trauma, and unhealthy ways of coping. It is okay to feel whatever it is that you are experiencing in any given moment. What's not okay is to stay locked into looping thoughts or a state of loneliness and pain.

The "gratitude effect" teaches us that it is possible to hold both joy *and* grief at the same time, that one can both mourn the loss of a loved one and still be grateful for all they brought to our lives. Gratitude practices, when done properly, teach us to hold both difficult emotions (like grief and sadness) and positive emotions (like love, joy, and connection) simultaneously. The point of practicing gratitude and positive thinking is to develop skills and strategies that prevent you from getting stuck in painful, *distorted* thinking patterns for long stretches of time while also cultivating more joy, satisfaction, and meaning in everyday life.

Optimism and Pessimism

While you may think you are either an optimist or pessimist, in truth, we each possess both qualities in varying proportions. Optimism is associated with the notion that experiences and events will likely have a positive outcome, and pessimism is associated with worries about the worst-case scenario.

Too much pessimism can result in unnecessary suffering, and too much optimism can lead to risky behaviors. Our survival and well-being depend upon finding a healthy balance between these two characteristics, which exist as a continuum within us. Research shows that our starting point on this continuum is at least partially inherited and is a manifestation of two basic drives—our drive to pursue rewards and our drive to avoid danger. Having an optimistic outlook is associated with persistence and adaptability in pursuing rewards; optimists try harder to achieve their goals, and they're less likely to experience depression or anxiety.

The pessimist, on the other hand, focuses on the dangers and pitfalls and holds little hope for the future. As a result, the pessimist tends to remain passive when faced with a challenge, as they believe the result will likely be a failure anyway. Extreme pessimism is also associated with poorer health; one study found that optimistic people live an average of six to eight years longer than pessimistic people.

We know that because whatever we focus on becomes stronger, it behooves pessimists and other negative thinkers to train their brains to see the positive possibilities rather than focusing on the obstacles. It's not toxic positivity, but rather learning to see things from a different vantage point that leads to better results. With practice, it is possible to shift to a more optimistic perspective over time. Here are some tips to facilitate this:

- Commit to a daily gratitude practice.

- Use positive language rather than negative when expressing yourself—for example, instead of "I will not be unkind," you might simply say, "I choose to be kind."

- Surround yourself more often with positive or optimistic people.

- Connect with your spiritual source of strength.

- Keep an open mind for the unexpected.

- Consider the possibility that your goals and desires will work out.

- Know that setbacks are temporary, and your gratitude practice will ultimately set you up for success.

- Celebrate and savor your wins.

Reframing

Reframing is the key strategy used in cognitive behavioral therapy (CBT). It helps us move mental filters or biases (aka cognitive distortions) and negative thought patterns into a more useful and realistic way of thinking. By gradually replacing negative thoughts with more positive ones, we change the neural pathways associated with our thoughts. This helps us grow our positivity so it becomes more dominant and allows negative thoughts to recede.

When a negative thought comes up, especially a persistent one, practice this strategy:

1. Notice the thought. For example, "I'm going to fail at this."

2. Acknowledge the thought by saying to yourself, "I see you, but I'm not paying attention to you right now."

3. Reframe the negative thought. For example, "I will do my best."

Like any skill, reframing requires practice to learn and master. You don't have to commit to a specific time or place when you practice reframing. Thoughts are firing in our brains throughout the day and night. The idea is to catch negative or distorted thoughts—especially the repetitive ones—as soon as you become aware that they are active in your mind.

With practice, you'll become more sensitized to those times when you're slipping in to negative thinking. You might even discover that this is your default way of perceiving most situations. However, once you become tuned in to your process around negative thinking, you are in a better position to start reframing. The more often you intentionally reframe your thoughts and words, the more swiftly your brain will start integrating this more advantageous perspective.

Reframing Difficult Situations and Memories

Reframing can also involve thinking about a difficult situation and finding an upside to that scenario that you had not previously considered. For example, if I'm thinking, "I lost my job. Now I'm worried that I'm unemployable. I'm too old, young, or inexperienced. I won't be able to pay the rent," I've gone down the rabbit hole and settled on the worst-case scenario in my mind. Alternatively, I could reframe the situation like this: "I've been burned out for a while now, and I wasn't enjoying that job. This break will give me time to get my health back on track and reflect on what I really want to do next. There are many opportunities out there, and I believe I can find something that matters more to me and makes better use of my talents and abilities."

Reframing develops resiliency and flexibility of the mind. To reframe negative memories or situations, follow these instructions:

1. Take a few deep breaths to calm yourself.

2. Bring your awareness to negative thoughts and negative speech.

3. Identify these thoughts as they arise and notice the words you choose to use, either in the way you talk to yourself or in conversation with others.

4. Investigate these thoughts and statements. Examine the evidence and ask yourself objectively:

   • Is this true?
   • Is this helpful?
   • How am I feeling right now?
   • How can I view this in a more positive way that's still accurate?

5. Once you find a more positive and realistic vantage point from which to reframe this outlook., try to record these reframes in your journal.

6. Don't get bogged down if you can't find a reframe for a particular circumstance; come back to it later and continue with the next negative thought or statement.

When reframing a negative or difficult experience, it sometimes helps to recall a positive memory or a time when a tough situation worked out well. This can improve mood and the experience of happiness. It also reminds us that challenging circumstances can (and often do) have positive outcomes. For example, if I break up with a business or love partner, as painful as this might be, I can recall other times when a similar situation *has* worked out for the best. This gives more heft and relief to my positive reframe.

I've witnessed countless times when a patient recalls a negative memory, triggering sadness and stress, or aggravating pain. In most cases, it's best not to repeatedly recall and retell the negative memory, at least not without the support of a therapist or coach, as doing so strengthens that memory and can cause people to get stuck. On the other hand, reframing a negative memory (by finding a more positive perspective from which to view it) can also promote healing, strengthen resiliency, and protect us from past hurts or current challenges while also opening the gateway to better opportunities ahead.

My final advice? Don't keep repeating your negative stories, and if you can't resist doing so, get the support of someone who can help you find a more positive way to look at it.

Setting Intentions

Now that we've explored some of the challenges that keep us stuck in negative thinking and covered practical ways to overcome it, we can discuss one of my favorite methods for cultivating gratitude and promoting positive thinking—setting intentions.

An intention is a clear, simple, positive statement or phrase that captures something you wish to feel or experience. Rooted in the present, intentions are used as an anchor and a guidepost. Setting an intention begins with self-reflection to understand yourself better and access your deepest desires. With that knowledge, you can make a clear and deliberate choice about what you would like to happen. Every time you set an intention, you reinforce in your mind something that matters to you. For example, setting the intention to be grateful increases a person's likelihood of practicing gratitude tremendously.

Intention setting can take just a few seconds, or it can be meditated on for as long as you wish. Morning intentions set the tone for the day by encouraging you to stay aligned with your values and take responsibility for your actions. A simple and powerful tool for personal growth, setting daily intentions requires you to regularly check in with yourself to clarify what is most important to you that day.

Be aware of the distinction between setting intentions and setting goals. Intentions are personal commitments grounded in the present; they are fluid and focused on our way of being. Goals, on the other hand, are future-oriented and are more concerned with doing things. That said, they often work together. For instance, you may set an intention to feel a sense of accomplishment, and while the feeling itself does not have to be tied to a particular goal, a goal you have set may begin to feel more within reach.

To set an intention, follow these instructions:

1. Take several deep breaths. Your mind will be more receptive to suggestions after a brief relaxation or meditation, so if you have a few extra minutes, you may want to sit quietly first.

2. Check in with yourself to determine what you truly desire. The intentions you set are best when they come from your heart and resonate with you in a deep way. Just be sure to keep it real.

3. The language you use to establish your intention matters. Be clear, brief, positive, and present. It's best to make a simple positive statement in the first person based on the present moment. Using phrases like "I am," "I choose," "I commit," and "I intend" add an element of strength and clarity. If you can't find an intention that seems to resonate with you or if it doesn't feel authentic, start with something like, "Today, I choose to remain calm and present."

4. Activate your intention through practice. Take mini breaks throughout the day by first taking a few deep breaths and then repeating your intention to yourself.

You can change your intention as you often as you wish, or you can stick to one intention until you experience the desired effect. Setting daily intentions gets easier and more internalized with practice.

Examples of Intentions

Today, I am grateful for _____ .

Today, I invite love and joy into my life.

I choose to be grateful as I move through my day.

Today, I make choices and take actions that are true to who I am.

I honor my emotions.

Today, I choose to listen to my heart.

I choose to deepen my relationships today.

I allow myself to find joy and meaning today.

I commit to staying calm and present throughout this day.

This day, I choose to listen actively to others before chiming in.

I choose to be kind no matter what happens today.

Today, I commit to giving myself grace when needed.

Today, I commit to taking responsibility for my choices.

Today, I choose to be mindful in my communication with others.

I am loving and lovable.

Today, I commit to being patient with myself and others.

I choose to be courageous with my heart today.

I eat healthfully.

I make conscious choices.

I love wholeheartedly.

Today, I choose to be caring and kind with my loved ones.

Today, I commit to making a positive impact on other people's lives.

Today, I commit to doing my best.

I accept myself as enough.

I choose to be courageous and expand my horizons today.

Today, I commit to finding the best in others.

Today, I invite success and abundance into my life.

I assume others are doing the best they can with what they have.

I am always enough.

I commit to being successful today.

I have everything I need within me.

Today, I commit to controlling my mindset.

I choose my work ethic.

I choose joy, peace, and love.

I commit to being all I can be.

I choose to access the power within me.

Gratitude Practices and Prompts

As discussed earlier, gratitude practices often require only a few minutes, but when done regularly, they have the potential to improve your life significantly. The gratitude effect can diminish negativity, depression, anger, pain, and anxiety while improving your self-esteem, self-compassion, relationships, energy levels, and outlook.

As you quiet darker aspects of the mind, you simultaneously create more joy and meaning in moment-to-moment experiences. The rewards from just a few minutes of daily practice are cumulative, and when integrated into your day, gratitude practices also benefit those around you.

Living with Gratitude

Each of the following simple practices can be incorporated throughout your day and, of course, your life. When done with intention, they will boost your capacity to recognize the many good aspects of life and help you develop a more positive mindset.

- Be kind to others and look for the good in them.
- Look for the positive aspects of the various circumstances you experience.
- Thank others often, especially those who serve you.
- Express gratitude at meals, whether you are alone or with others.

- Tell friends, colleagues, and family members specifically what you appreciate about them.

- Practice random acts of kindness.

- Record a "win" every day. Think of something that went well for you and make a note of it. Celebrating small wins can increase happiness in a big way.

- Periodically scan your horizon for something you appreciate or feel grateful for. If you have time, journal about your observations. Journaling reinforces your experiences and embeds the gratitude effect in your brain more quickly.

Gratitude Meditation

A powerful way to build positivity is by practicing a "gratitude meditation." This practice can be woven into the busiest of schedules since it only takes a couple of minutes. When you do this regularly, you will build a repertoire of positive experiences to draw from and will likely discover that you look forward to this time each day.

1. Sit comfortably, feeling grounded in your seat, and close your eyes.

2. Take a few deep breaths to relax your mind and body.

3. Ask yourself, "What am I really grateful for?"

4. Take the first thought that comes to mind and expand upon that idea, allowing positive experiences and feelings to emerge. Continue to build upon this positive experience

by involving all your senses—taste, touch, sight, sound, and smell.

5. Savor this experience by allowing it to sink into the recesses of your mind and body.

6. Intensify this feeling with vivid imagery. Linger longer than usual to embed this gratitude experience in your brain.

Ho'oponopono

Ho'oponopono is an ancient Hawaiian practice of healing through forgiveness and gratitude. This practice helps release negativity from a relationship, allowing room for positive experiences and feelings. You can engage in this practice any time you wish to clear negativity within yourself or between yourself and another. While you can do this by visualizing the other person in your mind's eye, this practice is particularly powerful if you're able to make eye contact with them as you follow these four simple, but not easy, steps:

1. Apologize and take responsibility for whatever was lost or broken: "I'm sorry."

2. Ask for forgiveness: "Please forgive me."

3. Express your gratitude: "Thank you."

4. Speak from the heart: "I love you."

Ho'oponopono is said to rid the mind and body of heavy energy by allowing the practitioner to reflect, forgive, repent, and feel gratitude, along with other heart-centered emotions. If the damaged relationship is with yourself, you can gaze at yourself in the mirror and go through the steps: "I'm sorry. Please forgive me. Thank you. I love you."

Fifty Gratitude Prompts

Sometimes it can be difficult to pinpoint what you are grateful for because you feel stuck, have run out of ideas, or are just drawing a blank. If that's the case, use one or more of these journaling prompts to get your gratitude flowing:

1. What do you love about a dear friend? What are their best qualities?
2. Describe a time when you laughed uncontrollably.
3. Describe your favorite moment or time of day.
4. What's the best gift you have ever received? What made it the best?
5. Describe a random act of kindness you experienced.
6. What is one thing no one knows about you, but you wish they did?
7. What movie touched your heart most deeply? Why?
8. Describe someone you admire.
9. Has a walk in nature ever left a lasting impression? If so, describe it.
10. What are your greatest strengths and why do they matter? Write about each one separately.

11. What were the best qualities of your parent or caretaker, even if the relationship was or is challenging?

12. Describe something you did that made someone happy.

13. What usually elevates your spirit when you're feeling down?

14. What do you love most about the time you are living in and why?

15. Describe a physical activity that brings you joy.

16. What's your favorite hobby? What do you love about it?

17. Describe your best friend from childhood.

18. What was your favorite activity from childhood?

19. Describe a breakthrough moment you had as an adult.

20. Recall your first love or the love of your life. What positive thing stands out most about that relationship?

21. Describe a moment when you saw the big picture and were no longer stuck in the mundane.

22. Who influences you the most in life? Describe that person.

23. What do you do that makes you feel lighter?

24. What are you most grateful for in your daily life and why?

25. Describe a moment in which your heart filled with love.

26. What would you miss if it were no longer in your life?

27. What do you appreciate about your body? Describe those parts of you.

28. Describe a simple pleasure you experience daily.

29. What's your favorite meal?

30. Describe a breathtaking moment in your life.

31. Whose company do you enjoy most and why?

32. Describe your most treasured travel experience.

33. What excites you about the future?

34. Describe a special memory from childhood.

35. Recall a time when you felt lucky to be alive. What happened?

36. Who can you talk to who really listens?

37. What do you do for yourself that enriches your health?

38. Describe someone you had a negative impression of who turned out to be someone you wished to befriend. What was the turning point?

39. What teacher or mentor impacted you most and why?

40. What touched you the most in your all-time favorite book?

41. Describe something about your family life that you cherish.

42. What's the best memory you can recall from the last few years? Describe all the details.

43. What are you grateful for about where you live?

44. Describe the last time you helped someone solve a problem and how that felt for you.

45. Who consistently makes your life better? Describe that person.

46. Recall one of your ideas you are happy came to fruition. Describe it.

47. List five things in your immediate surroundings for which you are grateful.

48. Describe how your perspective changes when you focus on gratitude.

49. Express gratitude for having as much food as you need to keep you healthy.

50. Write a letter of thanks to someone who has made a difference in your life. If this person is still living, consider giving them the letter.

Section Two

90 Days
of
Positive
Journaling

66 Gratitude is fertilizer for the mind, spreading connections and improving its function in nearly every realm of experience."

—Robert Emmons, PhD, *psychology professor at University of California, Davis,* The Little Book of Gratitude

---

To maximize the gratitude effect, I encourage you to fill out one page of this gratitude journal every day. Be consistent and allow this practice to become a habit. If you miss a day or two, give yourself some grace and just get going again the next day.

When filling out the "What I'm Grateful For" section, try to list at least three things. Then, choose one of those things to describe in greater detail in the "A Moment to Savor" section.

If you have difficulty summoning up something to be grateful for on a particular day, refer to page 35. If you need help setting intentions, you can check out page 28 for ideas.

DATE:

Intention:

What I'm Grateful For:

A Moment to Savor:

Living in a state of gratitude is the gateway to grace.

—**Arianna Huffington**

Intention:

What I'm Grateful For:

A Moment to Savor:

Gratitude is an antidote to negative emotions, a neutralizer of envy, hostility, worry, and irritation. It is savoring; it is not taking things for granted; it is present-oriented.

—Sonja Lyubomirsky

DATE:

Intention:

What I'm Grateful For:

A Moment to Savor:

Happiness is not something readymade. It comes from your own actions.

—Dalai Lama XIV

DATE:

Intention:

What I'm Grateful For:

A Moment to Savor:

Wear gratitude like a cloak, and it will feed every corner of your life.

—Rumi

DATE:

Intention:

What I'm Grateful For:

A Moment to Savor:

At times, our own light goes out and is rekindled by a spark from another person. Each of us has cause to think with deep gratitude of those who have lighted the flame within us.

—Albert Schweitzer

DATE:

Intention:

What I'm Grateful For:

A Moment to Savor:

We can only be said to be alive in those moments when our hearts are conscious of our treasures.

—Thornton Wilder

Intention:

What I'm Grateful For:

A Moment to Savor:

Piglet noticed that even though he had a Very Small Heart, it could hold a rather large amount of Gratitude.

—A. A. Milne, *Winnie-the-Pooh*

Intention:

What I'm Grateful For:

A Moment to Savor:

The more grateful I am, the more beauty I see.

—**Mary Davis**

DATE:

Intention:

What I'm Grateful For:

A Moment to Savor:

Acknowledging the good that you already have in your life is the foundation for all abundance.

—Eckhart Tolle, *A New Earth*

Intention:

What I'm Grateful For:

A Moment to Savor:

When you are grateful, fear disappears, and abundance appears.

—Tony Robbins

Intention:

What I'm Grateful For:

A Moment to Savor:

What separates privilege from entitlement is gratitude.

—Brené Brown

DATE:

Intention:

What I'm Grateful For:

A Moment to Savor:

The more you express gratitude for what you have, the more likely you will have even more to express gratitude for.

—Zig Ziglar

DATE:

Intention:

What I'm Grateful For:

A Moment to Savor:

The best way to find yourself is to lose yourself in the service of others.

—Mahatma Gandhi

DATE:

Intention:

What I'm Grateful For:

A Moment to Savor:

Expectation has brought me disappointment. Disappointment has brought me wisdom. Acceptance, gratitude and appreciation have brought me joy and fulfillment.

—Rasheed Ogunlaru

DATE:

Intention:

What I'm Grateful For:

A Moment to Savor:

More Miracles occur from Gratitude and Forgiveness than anything else.

—**Philip H. Friedman,** *The Forgiveness Solution*

DATE:

Intention:

What I'm Grateful For:

A Moment to Savor:

Gratitude is not only the greatest of virtues, but the parent of all others.

—Marcus Tullius Cicero

Intention:

What I'm Grateful For:

A Moment to Savor:

When we are no longer able to change a situation, we are challenged to change ourselves.

—**Viktor E. Frankl,** *Man's Search for Meaning*

DATE:

Intention:

_____
_____

What I'm Grateful For:

_____
_____
_____
_____
_____
_____
_____

A Moment to Savor:

_____
_____
_____
_____
_____
_____
_____

Gratitude will shift you to a higher frequency, and you will attract much better things.

—Rhonda Byrne

DATE:

Intention:

What I'm Grateful For:

A Moment to Savor:

Let us rise up and be thankful, for if we didn't learn a lot today, at least we learned a little, and if we didn't learn a little, at least we didn't get sick, and if we got sick, at least we didn't die; so, let us all be thankful.

—Leo Buscaglia, *Born for Love*

Intention:

What I'm Grateful For:

A Moment to Savor:

When it comes to life the critical thing is whether you take things for granted or take them with gratitude.

—G. K. Chesterton

DATE:

Intention:

What I'm Grateful For:

A Moment to Savor:

Gratitude makes sense of our past, brings peace for today, and creates a vision for tomorrow.

—Melody Beattie

DATE:

Intention:

What I'm Grateful For:

A Moment to Savor:

Thankfulness is the beginning of gratitude. Gratitude is the completion of thankfulness. Thankfulness may consist merely of words. Gratitude is shown in acts.

—Henri Frederic Amiel

DATE:

Intention:

What I'm Grateful For:

A Moment to Savor:

This is a wonderful day. I have never seen this one before.

—Maya Angelou

Intention:

What I'm Grateful For:

A Moment to Savor:

The soul that gives thanks can find comfort in everything; the soul that complains can find comfort in nothing.

—Hannah Whitall Smith

DATE:

Intention:

What I'm Grateful For:

A Moment to Savor:

By taking just a few extra seconds to stay with a positive experience—even the comfort in a single breath—you'll help turn a passing mental state into lasting neural structure.

—Rick Hanson, *Hardwiring Happiness*

Intention:

What I'm Grateful For:

A Moment to Savor:

Do not spoil what you have by desiring what you have not; remember that what you now have was once among the things you only hoped for.

—Epicurus

Intention:

What I'm Grateful For:

A Moment to Savor:

When I started counting my blessings, my whole life turned around.

—Willie Nelson

Intention:

What I'm Grateful For:

A Moment to Savor:

It's a funny thing about life, once you begin to take note of the things you are grateful for, you begin to lose sight of the things that you lack.

—Germany Kent

Intention:

What I'm Grateful For:

A Moment to Savor:

No duty is more urgent than giving thanks.

—James Allen

DATE:

Intention:

What I'm Grateful For:

A Moment to Savor:

The trouble is, you think you have time.

—**Jack Kornfield,** *Buddha's Little Instruction Book*

DATE:

Intention:

_____

_____

What I'm Grateful For:

_____

_____

_____

_____

_____

_____

A Moment to Savor:

_____

_____

_____

_____

_____

_____

_____

When eating fruit, remember the one who planted the tree.

—Vietnamese proverb

DATE:

Intention:

What I'm Grateful For:

A Moment to Savor:

Appreciation is a wonderful thing. It makes what is excellent in others belong to us as well.

—Voltaire

DATE:

Intention:

What I'm Grateful For:

A Moment to Savor:

When we focus on our gratitude, the tide of disappointment goes out and the tide of love rushes in.

—Kristin Armstrong

DATE:

Intention:

What I'm Grateful For:

A Moment to Savor:

Happiness cannot be traveled to, owned, earned, worn, or consumed. Happiness is the spiritual experience of living every minute with love, grace, and gratitude.

—Denis Waitley

DATE:

Intention:

What I'm Grateful For:

A Moment to Savor:

In ordinary life, we hardly realize that we receive a great deal more than we give, and that it is only with gratitude that life becomes rich.

—Dietrich Bonhoeffer

DATE:

Intention:

What I'm Grateful For:

A Moment to Savor:

My expectations were reduced to zero when I was 21. Everything since then has been a bonus.

—Stephen W. Hawking

Intention:

What I'm Grateful For:

A Moment to Savor:

When you arise in the morning, think of what a precious privilege it is to be alive—to breathe, to think, to enjoy, to love—then make that day count!

—Marcus Aurelius

Intention:

What I'm Grateful For:

A Moment to Savor:

As we express our gratitude, we must never forget that the highest appreciation is not to utter words, but to live by them.

—John F. Kennedy

DATE:

Intention:

What I'm Grateful For:

A Moment to Savor:

Gratitude looks to the Past and love to the Present; fear, avarice, lust, and ambition look ahead.

—**C. S. Lewis,** *The Screwtape Letters*

Intention:

What I'm Grateful For:

A Moment to Savor:

The highest tribute to the dead is not grief but gratitude.

—Thornton Wilder

Intention:

What I'm Grateful For:

A Moment to Savor:

Not what we say about our blessings, but how we use them, is the true measure of our thanksgiving.

—W. T. Purkiser

DATE:

Intention:

What I'm Grateful For:

A Moment to Savor:

Feeling gratitude and not expressing it is like wrapping a present and not giving it.

—William Arthur Ward

DATE:

Intention:

What I'm Grateful For:

A Moment to Savor:

The miracle is not to walk on water. The miracle is to walk on the green earth, dwelling deeply in the present moment and feeling truly alive.

—Thich Nhat Hanh

DATE:

Intention:

What I'm Grateful For:

A Moment to Savor:

The most beautiful moments in life are moments when you are expressing your joy, not when you are seeking it.

—**Jaggi Vasudev**

Intention:

What I'm Grateful For:

A Moment to Savor:

A grateful mindset can set you free from the prison of disempowerment and the shackles of misery.

—**Steve Maraboli,** *Unapologetically You*

DATE:

Intention:

What I'm Grateful For:

A Moment to Savor:

Gratitude bestows reverence . . . changing forever how we experience life and the world.

—John Milton

Intention:

What I'm Grateful For:

A Moment to Savor:

It's up to us to choose contentment and thankfulness now—and to stop imagining that we have to have everything perfect before we'll be happy.

—**Joanna Gaines,** *The Magnolia Story*

DATE:

Intention:

What I'm Grateful For:

A Moment to Savor:

Those who are not grateful soon begin to complain of everything.

—**Thomas Merton,** *Thoughts in Solitude*

Intention:

What I'm Grateful For:

A Moment to Savor:

Joy is the simplest form of gratitude.

—**Karl Barth**

Intention:

What I'm Grateful For:

A Moment to Savor:

Sometimes the bad things that happen in our lives put us directly on the path to the best things that will ever happen to us.

—Nicole Reed, *Ruining You*

DATE:

Intention:

What I'm Grateful For:

A Moment to Savor:

I promise if you keep searching for everything beautiful in the world, you will eventually become it.

—Tyler Kent White

Intention:

What I'm Grateful For:

A Moment to Savor:

Remember that sometimes not getting what you want is a wonderful stroke of luck.

—**Dalai Lama XIV**

DATE:

Intention:

What I'm Grateful For:

A Moment to Savor:

Happiness is letting go of what you think your life is supposed to look like and celebrating it for everything that it is.

—Mandy Hale

DATE:

Intention:

_____

_____

What I'm Grateful For:

_____

_____

_____

_____

_____

_____

_____

A Moment to Savor:

_____

_____

_____

_____

_____

_____

Love wholeheartedly, be surprised, give thanks and praise—then you will discover the fullness of your life.

—David Steindl-Rast

Intention:

What I'm Grateful For:

A Moment to Savor:

If you concentrate on finding whatever is good in every situation, you will discover that your life will suddenly be filled with gratitude, a feeling that nurtures the soul.

—Harold S. Kushner

Intention:

What I'm Grateful For:

A Moment to Savor:

Don't fear failure so much that you refuse to try new things. The saddest summary of a life contains three descriptions: could have, might have, and should have.

—Louis E. Boone

Intention:

What I'm Grateful For:

A Moment to Savor:

Humility is not thinking less of yourself, it's thinking of yourself less.

—**Rick Warren,** *The Purpose-Driven Life*

DATE:

Intention:

What I'm Grateful For:

A Moment to Savor:

You need to be aware of what others are doing, applaud their efforts, acknowledge their successes, and encourage them in their pursuits. When we all help one another, everybody wins.

—Jim Stovall

Intention:

What I'm Grateful For:

A Moment to Savor:

Enjoy the little things, for one day you may look back and realize they were the big things.

—Robert Brault

DATE:

Intention:

What I'm Grateful For:

A Moment to Savor:

Have gratitude for the things you're discarding. By giving gratitude, you're giving closure to the relationship with that object, and by doing so, it becomes a lot easier to let go.

—Marie Kondo

Intention:

What I'm Grateful For:

A Moment to Savor:

Whatever we are waiting for—peace of mind, contentment, grace, the inner awareness of simple abundance—it will surely come to us, but only when we are ready to receive it with an open and grateful heart.

—**Sarah Ban Breathnach**

Intention:

What I'm Grateful For:

A Moment to Savor:

Great things happen to those who don't stop believing, trying, learning, and being grateful.

—**Roy T. Bennett,** *The Light in the Heart*

DATE:

Intention:

What I'm Grateful For:

A Moment to Savor:

Every sunset is an opportunity to reset. Every sunrise begins with new eyes.

—Richie Norton

DATE:

Intention:

What I'm Grateful For:

A Moment to Savor:

The best way to cheer yourself is to try to cheer someone else up.

—Mark Twain

Intention:

What I'm Grateful For:

A Moment to Savor:

Breathe. Let go. And remind yourself that this very moment is the only one you know you have for sure.

—Oprah Winfrey

DATE:

Intention:

What I'm Grateful For:

A Moment to Savor:

Sometimes we spend so much time and energy thinking about where we want to go that we don't notice where we happen to be.

—**Dan Gutman,** *From Texas with Love*

Intention:

What I'm Grateful For:

A Moment to Savor:

Don't pray when it rains if you don't pray when the sun shines.

—Leroy "Satchel" Paige

Intention:

What I'm Grateful For:

A Moment to Savor:

If you believe it will work out, you'll see opportunities. If you believe it won't, you'll see obstacles.

—**Wayne W. Dyer**

DATE:

Intention:

What I'm Grateful For:

A Moment to Savor:

If you wish to be happy, you can begin by thinking, "Everybody has something good in him; there is something that I can learn from every human being."

—Dada J. P. Vaswani

DATE:

Intention:

What I'm Grateful For:

A Moment to Savor:

Now is no time to think of what you do not have. Think of what you can do with what there is.

—**Ernest Hemingway,** *The Old Man and the Sea*

Intention:

What I'm Grateful For:

A Moment to Savor:

There is a calmness to a life lived in gratitude, a quiet joy.

—**Ralph H. Blum**

DATE:

Intention:

What I'm Grateful For:

A Moment to Savor:

No one who achieves success does so without the help of others. The wise and confident acknowledge this help with gratitude.

—Alfred North Whitehead

DATE:

Intention:

What I'm Grateful For:

A Moment to Savor:

Forget yesterday—it has already forgotten you. Don't sweat tomorrow—you haven't even met. Instead, open your eyes and your heart to a truly precious gift—today.

—**Steve Maraboli,** *Life, the Truth, and Being Free*

DATE:

Intention:

What I'm Grateful For:

A Moment to Savor:

Gratitude also opens your eyes to the limitless potential of the universe, while dissatisfaction closes your eyes to it.

—Stephen Richards

Intention:

What I'm Grateful For:

A Moment to Savor:

Though no one can go back and make a brand-new start, anyone can start from now and make a brand-new ending.

—Carl Bard

Intention:

What I'm Grateful For:

A Moment to Savor:

To make a difference in someone's life, you don't have to be brilliant, rich, beautiful, or perfect. You just have to care.

—Mandy Hale

DATE:

Intention:

What I'm Grateful For:

A Moment to Savor:

Decide what kind of life you actually want, then say no to everything that isn't that.

—Unknown

DATE:

Intention:

_____

_____

What I'm Grateful For:

_____

_____

_____

_____

_____

_____

A Moment to Savor:

_____

_____

_____

_____

_____

_____

Happiness is not something you postpone for the future; it is something you design for the present.

—**Jim Rohn**

Intention:

What I'm Grateful For:

A Moment to Savor:

Unexpected kindness is the most powerful, least costly, and most underrated agent of human change.

—Bob Kerrey

DATE:

Intention:

What I'm Grateful For:

A Moment to Savor:

Gratitude is when memory is stored in the heart and not in the mind.

—Lionel Hampton

DATE:

Intention:

What I'm Grateful For:

A Moment to Savor:

I don't have to chase extraordinary moments to find happiness—it's right in front of me if I'm paying attention and practicing gratitude.

—Brené Brown

DATE:

Intention:

What I'm Grateful For:

A Moment to Savor:

Some people are always grumbling because roses have thorns; I am thankful that thorns have roses.

—Jean-Baptiste Alphonse Karr

DATE:

Intention:

What I'm Grateful For:

A Moment to Savor:

"Thank you" is the best prayer that anyone could say. I say that one a lot. Thank you expresses extreme gratitude, humility, understanding.

—Alice Walker

DATE:

Intention:

What I'm Grateful For:

A Moment to Savor:

The best and most beautiful things in this world cannot be seen nor even touched, but only just felt in the heart.

—Anne Sullivan

Intention:

What I'm Grateful For:

A Moment to Savor:

When some things go wrong, take a moment to be thankful for the many things that are going right.

—Annie Gottlier

DATE:

Intention:

What I'm Grateful For:

A Moment to Savor:

Instead of thinking "I will be happy when," try thinking "I will be happy now."

—Unknown

Intention:

What I'm Grateful For:

A Moment to Savor:

Gratitude is a powerful catalyst for happiness. It's the spark that lights a fire of joy in your soul.

—**Amy Collette,** *The Gratitude Connection*

Intention:

What I'm Grateful For:

A Moment to Savor:

You have to participate relentlessly in the manifestation of your own blessings.

—**Elizabeth Gilbert,** *Eat, Pray, Love*

DATE:

Intention:

What I'm Grateful For:

A Moment to Savor:

Gratitude opens the door to the power, the wisdom, the creativity of the universe. You open the door through gratitude.

—Deepak Chopra

DATE:

Intention:

What I'm Grateful For:

A Moment to Savor:

Cultivate the habit of being grateful for every good thing that comes to you, and to give thanks continuously. And because all things have contributed to your advancement, you should include all things in your gratitude.

—Ralph Waldo Emerson

Suggested Reading

Art of Living, The: Peace and Freedom in the Here and Now, reprint edition, by Thich Nhat Hanh (HarperOne, 2023).

Buddha's Brain: The Practical Neuroscience of Happiness, Love & Wisdom by Rick Hanson (New Harbinger Publications, 2009).

Daily Stoic, The: 366 Meditations on Wisdom, Perseverance, and the Art of Living by Ryan Holiday and Stephen Hanselman (Portfolio, 2016).

Flow: The Psychology of Optimal Experience by Mihaly Csikszentmihalyi (Harper Perennial Modern Classics, 2008).

Good Business: Leadership, Flow, and the Making of Meaning, reprint edition, by Mihaly Csikszentmihalyi (Penguin Books, 2004).

Gratitude by Oliver Sacks (Knopf, 2015).

Gratitude: A Way of Life by Louise Hay (Hay House, 1996).

Hardwiring Happiness: The New Brain Science of Contentment, Calm, and Confidence, reprint edition, by Rick Hanson (Harmony, 2016).

Help, Thanks, Wow by Anne Lamott (Riverhead Books, 2012).

Learned Optimism: How to Change Your Mind and Your Life, reprint edition, by Martin E. P. Seligman (Vintage, 2006).

Living with Joy: Keys to Personal Power and Spiritual Transformation, 25th Anniversary Edition, by Sanaya Roman (HJ Kramer/New World Library, 2011).

Miracle of Mindfulness, The: An Introduction to the Practice of Meditation by Thich Nhat Hanh (Beacon Press, 1999).

Power of Intention, The, by Dr. Wayne W. Dyer (Hay House, 2005).

Power of Letting Go, The: How to Drop Everything That's Holding You Back by John Purkiss (Aster, 2020).

Think Like a Monk: Train Your Mind for Peace and Purpose Every Day, illustrated edition, by Jay Shetty (Simon & Schuster, 2020).

References

Achor, Shawn, and Michelle Gielan. "Consuming Negative News Can Make You Less Effective at Work." *Harvard Business Review*. September 14, 2015. https://hbr.org/2015/09/consuming-negative-news-can-make-you-less-effective-at-work.

Achor, Shawn. "Positive Intelligence." *Harvard Business Review*. January–February 2012. https://hbr.org/2012/01/positive-intelligence.

Allen, Summer. "The Science of Gratitude." The Greater Good Science Center at UC Berkeley. May 2018. https://ggsc.berkeley.edu/images/uploads/GGSC-JTF_White_Paper-Gratitude-FINAL.pdf?_ga=2.82610261.2142947331.1637096170-1362583773.1634590861.

Bates, Timothy C. "The Glass Is Half Full and Half Empty: A Population-Representative Twin Study Testing If Optimism and Pessimism Are Distinct Systems." *Journal of Positive Psychology* 10, no. 6 (November 2015): 533–542. https://doi.org/10.1080/17439760.2015.1015155.

Bevan, Keri. "Ho'oponopono: A Journey to Inner Freedom." *The Daily Dish*. February 8, 2023. https://dailydish.co.uk/hooponopono-a-journey-to-inner-freedom.

Blades, Robin. "Protecting the Brain against Bad News." *Canadian Medical Association Journal* 193, no. 12 (March 2021): E428—E429. https://doi.org/10.1503/cmaj.1095928.

Bouchrika, Imed. "35 Scientific Benefits of Gratitude: Mental Health Research Findings." Research.com. June 27, 2023. https://research.com/education/scientific-benefits-of-gratitude.

Brown, Joshua, and Joel Wong. "How Gratitude Changes You and Your Brain." *Greater Good Magazine*. June 6, 2017. https://greatergood.berkeley.edu/article/item/how_gratitude_changes_you_and_your_brain.

Burton, Linda Roszak. "The Neuroscience of Gratitude." Wharton Health Care Management Alumni Association. Accessed July 6, 2023. https://www.whartonhealthcare.org/the_neuroscience_of_gratitude.

Chopra, Deepak, and Kabir Sehgal. "Being a Pessimist Is Bad for Your Health and Brain—Here's What to Do about It." *CNBC*. Last modified September 9, 2019. https://www.cnbc.com/2019/07/08/deepak-chopra-being-a-pessimist-can-prevent-longer-life-and-healthier-brain.html.

Chowdhury, Madhuleena Roy. "The Neuroscience of Gratitude and Effects on the Brain." *Positive Psychology*. April 9, 2019. https://positivepsychology.com/neuroscience-of-gratitude.

Cregg, David R., and Jennifer S. Cheavens. "Gratitude Interventions: Effective Self-Help? A Meta-Analysis of the Impact on Symptoms of Depression and Anxiety." *Journal of Happiness Studies* 22, no. 1 (January 2021): 413–445. https://doi.org/10.1007/s10902-020-00236-6.

Dana, Deb. *The Polyvagal Theory in Therapy*. New York: W. W. Norton and Company, 2018.

Fox, Glenn R., Jonas Kaplan, Hanna Damasio, and Antonio Damasio. "Neural Correlates of Gratitude." *Frontiers in Psychology* 6, article 1491 (September 2015). https://psycnet.apa.org/record/2016-20151-001.

"Happy Workers Are 13% More Productive." University of Oxford. October 24, 2019. https://www.ox.ac.uk/news/2019-10-24-happy-workers-are-13-more-productive.

Hartman, Taylor. "How Practicing Gratitude Can Rewire Your Brain." *SageMED*. May 1, 2020. https://www.sagemed.co/blog/how-practicing-gratitude-can-rewire-your-brain.

Harvard Medical School. "Giving Thanks Can Make You Happier." *Harvard Health Publishing*. August 14, 2021. https://www.health.harvard.edu/healthbeat/giving-thanks-can-make-you-happier.

Harvard Medical School. "Optimism and Your Health." *Harvard Health Publishing*. May 1, 2008. https://www.health.harvard.edu/heart-health/optimism-and-your-health.

Harvard University Stress & Development Lab. "Positive Reframing and Examining the Evidence." Harvard University. Accessed July 6, 2023. https://sdlab.fas.harvard.edu/cognitive-reappraisal/positive-reframing-and-examining-evidence.

Hecht, David. "The Neural Basis of Optimism and Pessimism." *Experimental Neurobiology* 22, no. 3 (September 2013): 173–199. https://doi.org/10.5607/en.2013.22.3.173.

Iati, Marisa. "Here's a New Reason to Be an Optimist: You'll Live Longer, Study Says." *The Washington Post*. August 29, 2019. https://www.washingtonpost.com/lifestyle/2019/08/29/heres-new-reason-be-an-optimist-youre-likely-live-longer-study-says.

Koga, Hayami K., Claudia Trudel-Fitzgerald, Lewina O. Lee, Peter James, Candyce Kroenke, Lorena Garcia, and Aladdin H. Shadyab, et al. "Optimism, Lifestyle, and Longevity in a Racially Diverse Cohort of Women." *Journal of the American Geriatrics Society* 70, no. 10 (June 2022): 2793–2804. https://doi.org/10.1111/jgs.17897.

Lee, Lewina O., Peter James, Emily S. Zevon, and Laura D. Kubzansky. "Optimism Is Associated with Exceptional Longevity in 2 Epidemiologic Cohorts of Men and Women." *Proceedings of the National Academy of Sciences of the United States of America* 116, no. 37 (August 2019): 18357–18362. https://doi.org/10.1073/pnas.1900712116.

Lindberg, Eric. "Practicing Gratitude Can Have Profound Health Benefits, USC Experts Say." *USC News.* November 25, 2019. https://news.usc.edu/163123/gratitude-health-research-thanksgiving-usc-experts/.

McCraty, Rollin, and Doc Childre. "The Grateful Heart: The Psychophysiology of Appreciation." In *The Psychology of Gratitude*, edited by R. A. Emmons & M. E. McCullough, 230–55. New York: Oxford University Press, 2004.

Motamed-Jahromi, Mohadeseh, Zhila Fereidouni, and Azizallah Dehghan. "Effectiveness of Positive Thinking Training Program on Nurses' Quality of Work Life through Smartphone Applications." *International Scholarly Research Notices* (May 2017): 4965816. https://doi.org/10.1155/2017/4965816.

National Institute on Aging. "Optimism Linked to Longevity and Well-Being in Two Recent Studies." National Institutes of Health. December 8, 2022. https://www.nia.nih.gov/news/optimism-linked-longevity-and-well-being-two-recent-studies.

NeuroHealth Associates. "Neuroscience Reveals: Gratitude Literally Rewires Your Brain to be Happier." *NeuroHealth*. July 4, 2020. https://nhahealth.com/neuroscience-reveals-gratitude-literally-rewires-your-brain-to-be-happier.

"Optimism and Pessimism." Psychology.iresearch.net. Accessed July 6, 2023. http://psychology.iresearchnet.com/counseling-psychology/personality-traits/optimism-and-pessimism-counseling.

P., Gene. "Benefits of Gratitude: 31 Powerful Reasons to be More Grateful." *Happier Human*. March 17, 2023. https://www.happierhuman.com/benefits-of-gratitude.

Parker, Clifton B. "Embracing Stress Is More Important than Reducing Stress, Stanford Psychologist Says." *Stanford News*. May 7, 2015. https://news.stanford.edu/2015/05/07/stress-embrace-mcgonigal-050715.

Rice, Andrea. "Rewiring Your Brain for Positivity with 'Mature Gratitude.'" *PsychCentral*. Accessed July 6, 2023. https://psychcentral.com/health/rewiring-your-brain-for-positivity-with-gratitude.

Sansone, Randy A., and Lori A. Sansone. "Gratitude and Well Being: The Benefits of Appreciation." *Psychiatry (Edgmont)* 7, no. 11 (November 2010): 18–22. https://www.ncbi.nlm.nih.gov/pmc/articles/PMC3010965.

Stillman, Jessica. "3 Reasons You Should Quit Following the News." *Inc.* December 19, 2016. https://www.inc.com/jessica-stillman/3-reasons-you-should-quit-following-the-news.html.

Stillman, Jessica. "The Science of Why You Really Shouldn't Start Your Day with the Headlines." *Inc.* October 31, 2017. https://www.inc.com/jessica-stillman/the-science-of-why-you-really-shouldnt-start-your-day-with-headlines.html.

Tenney, Elizabeth R., Jared M. Poole, and Ed Diener. "Does Positivity Enhance Work Performance?: Why, When, and What We Don't Know." *Research in Organizational Behavior* 36 (November 2016): 27–46. https://doi.org/10.1016/j.riob.2016.11.002.

Trafton, Anne. "A Delicate Balance between Positive and Negative Emotion: Neuroscientists Identify Two Neuron Populations That Encode Happy or Fearful Memories." *MIT News*. October 17, 2016. https://news.mit.edu/2016/two-neuron-populations-encode-happy-fearful-memories-1017.

Trafton, Anne. "Scientists Identify Brain Circuit That Drives Pleasure-Inducing Behavior: Surprisingly, the Neurons Are Located in a Brain Region Thought to Be Linked with Fear." *MIT News*. March 22, 2017. https://news.mit.edu/2017/brain-circuit-pleasure-inducing-behavior-0322.

Wilson, Jane Taylor. "Brightening the Mind: The Impact of Practicing Gratitude on Focus and Resilience in Learning." *Journal of the Scholarship of Teaching and Learning* 16, no. 4 (August 2016): 1–13. https://doi.org/10.14434/josotl.v16i4.19998.

Whitfield, John B., Gu Zhu, J. George Landers, and Nicholas G. Martin. "Pessimism Is Associated with Greater All-Cause and Cardiovascular Mortality, but Optimism Is Not Protective." *Scientific Reports* 10 (July 2020): 12609. https://doi.org/10.1038/s41598-020-69388-y.

Wood, Alex M., Stephen Joseph, Joanna Lloyd, and Samuel Atkins. "Gratitude Influences Sleep through the Mechanism of Pre-Sleep Cognitions." *Journal of Psychosomatic Research* 66, no. 1 (January 2009): 43–48. https://doi.org/10.1016/j.jpsychores.2008.09.002.

School. She trained faculty, staff, and students to manage stress, pain, and psychosomatic disorders while improving resiliency, communication, and leadership abilities.

Dr. Kamen continues to lead global online programs, workshops, and retreats for corporations, hospitals, and academic institutions. She weaves together evidence-based skills and strategies for mind management, self-regulation, healthy relationships, and living one's personal vision. Dr. Kamen uses the Thera-Coaching process to help individuals gain understanding and resolution with their past in the service of moving forward and cultivating an intentional and purpose-driven life.

Dr. Kamen divides her time between her two favorite islands: Martha's Vineyard and New York City. She cherishes her time with her two adult children and their budding families. For more information, visit DrRandyKamen.com.

Hi there,

We hope you enjoyed *The Gratitude Effect Positivity Journal*. If you have any questions or concerns about your book, or have received a damaged copy, please contact customerservice@penguinrandomhouse.com. We're here and happy to help.

Also, please consider writing a review on your favorite retailer's website to let others know what you thought of the book!

Sincerely,
The Zeitgeist Team

About the Author

Randy E. Kamen, EdD, is a psychologist, coach, educator, and author of *Behind the Therapy Door: Simple Strategies to Transform Your Life*. Her aim is to help people embody their inner wisdom and leadership skills in both the personal and professional arenas. She pioneered new territory in mind-body medicine and positive psychology at Boston University's School of Medicine and Dentistry and Harvard Medical